Glass

Edited by Rebecca Stefoff

Text © 1991 by Garrett Educational Corporation

First Published in the United States in 1991
by Garrett Educational Corporation,
130 East 13th, Ada, Oklahoma 74820

First Published in 1987 by A & C Black (Publishers) Limited, London
with the title GLASS
© 1987 A & C Black (Publishers) Ltd.

Manufactured in the United States of America

Library of Congress Cataloging in Publication Data

Chandler, Jane.
    Glass / Jane Chandler ; photographs by Ed Barber.
    p.   cm.—(Threads)
    "First published in 1987 by A & C Black (Publishers) Limited,
London with the title Glass"—Copr. page.
    Summary: Discusses glass, its manufacture, uses, and variety.
    ISBN 1-56074-004-3
    1. Glass—Juvenile literature.   [1. Glass.]
I. Barber, Ed. ill.   II. Title.   III. Series.
TP857.3.C42   1991
666'.1—dc20   91-18191
                                                                    CIP
                                                                    AC

Glass

Jane Chandler

Photographs by Ed Barber

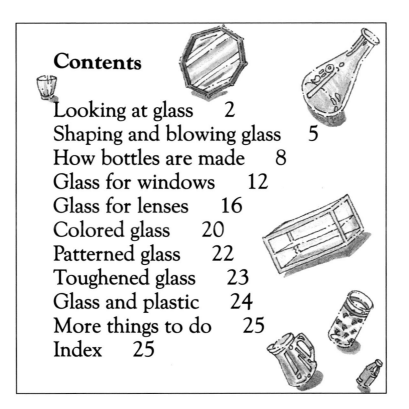

Contents

Craven-Pamlico-Carteret
Regional Library

GEC GARRETT EDUCATIONAL CORPORATION

Looking at glass

What does the word
"glass" make you
think of? A window?
A glass for drinking?

Have a look at this picture and see if you can spot the things that are made from glass.

Did you find these in the picture?

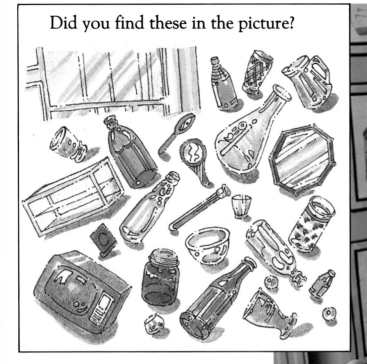

Glass comes in all different shapes and sizes.

Have a closer look at some things made of glass.
Be *very* careful with them. Glass can break easily and broken glass is sharp and dangerous. Make sure that there is an adult nearby to help you.

Try looking through some glass objects. Can you see through them? Things that we can see through are called transparent.

Feel the glass with your fingers. Is it rough or smooth? Glass feels hard; it doesn't bend or stretch. How do you think it can be made into so many different shapes and sizes?

4

Shaping and blowing glass

These bits of broken glass are going to be made into new shapes.

First, they are put into a very hot oven, called a furnace. Inside the furnace, the bits of broken glass will melt together into a thick liquid. Glass like this is called molten glass and it can be shaped, pulled, and stretched.

The glassmaker uses a special iron tube to take a blob of molten glass out of the furnace.

He shapes the glass by rolling it along a piece of paper.

Then he starts to blow down the tube into the glass, like blowing up a balloon. Can you see that the glass is beginning to be blown outwards?

The glassmaker keeps shaping and blowing the glass until he has made the shape he wants. He might also add some color to the glass while it is hot.

This glass bowl is nearly ready and the glassmaker is cutting a hole in the top.

Then he spins the bowl round and round by rolling the rod along his bench. Slowly the bowl begins to flatten out.

When he has finished, the glassmaker carefully breaks off the iron tube and leaves the bowl to cool.

Until a few hundred years ago, all glass was blown and shaped by hand, and glass was very expensive. Nowadays, most glass is shaped by machines in factories, but some very beautiful and expensive glass objects are still made in this old-fashioned way.

How bottles are made

Have you ever taken your old bottles to a recycling center?

After a few days, your bottles will be taken by truck to a factory and recycled (made into new bottles).

At the factory, the bottles are loaded on to a conveyor belt and broken into small pieces by a crusher.

The crushed glass goes over a huge strainer. You can see it in this picture. Only the small bits of glass fall through the strainer. They will be used to make new bottles. The old bottle-tops, corks and bits of plastic are sucked up by machines like big vacuum cleaners, or picked up by magnets. The clean glass is ready to be melted down in the furnace.

New bottles are made from a mixture of recycled glass and new glass that is made at the factory.

The new glass is made from three different ingredients. Here they are being pushed into the furnace. The most important ingredient is a very pure, clean kind of sand, called silica. The other two ingredients are soda and lime. Soda makes the sand melt more easily in the furnace and lime makes the glass hard and waterproof. Glass made only from sand and soda would dissolve in water.

Glass made from these three ingredients is called "soda-lime-silica glass."

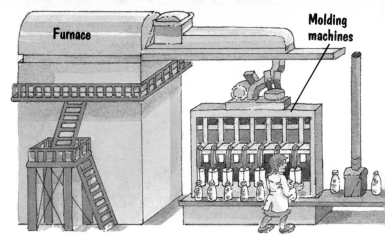

Inside the furnace, the temperature is about six times hotter than you can set your oven at home. The recycled glass and the ingredients for the new glass are all melted together.

1. The molten glass moves down tubes to the molding machine. As it oozes out of the tubes, it is cut into blobs by a hunge pair of scissors.

2. Each blob of glass slides down another tube and into a mold at the bottom.

The inside of each mold is shaped like a bottle or a jar. When air is blown into the mold, the glass is pushed into the shape of the mold, like this,

Bottle shaped

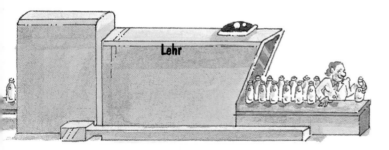

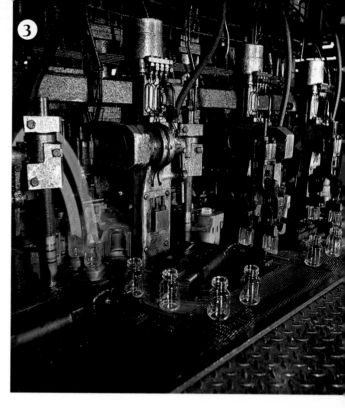

3. Then the red-hot bottles and jars are lifted out of the molds and sent down a conveyor belt into a long tunnel, called a lehr.

In the lehr, the glass is heated up again and then cooled very slowly. If the glass is cooled too quickly, it may break easily later on.

4. This man is checking the bottles as they come out of the lehr. He makes sure that none of them are broken or the wrong shape.

When the bottles have been checked, they are ready to be labelled and used.

11

Glass for windows

Glass can be made into flat pieces as well as bottles and containers.

Have you ever seen a store window being put in?

Big pieces of glass for windows have to be perfectly flat and smooth. They are called float glass because of the way they are made. When the glass has been melted in the furnace, it is floated on top of another liquid to make a flat layer.

If you want to see how it works, try this.

You will need

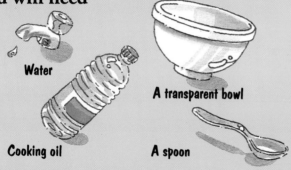

Water

A transparent bowl

Cooking oil

A spoon

How to do it

Fill the bowl about half full of water.
Then gently pour the oil over the back
of a spoon, on to the top of the water.
Can you see how a layer of oil floats on
top of the water?

Molten glass can't be
floated on water. Instead,
the glass is floated on
metal that is so hot that it
has turned to liquid.

The layer of molten glass
is then cooled very slowly
and comes out in big flat
pieces like this. Then the
glass is washed and cut up
into smaller pieces.

Have a look at some different kinds of windows.
Draw the different shapes and look through
the glass.

▲ Window panes like these don't need to be as big
and flat as store windows. They are called sheet
glass and are made in a factory. Sheet glass is made
by pulling a long ribbon of molten glass out of the
furnace. It's a bit like dipping a spoon into some
hot fudge sauce and pulling out a long strand.

◀ Before glass was made in factories, window panes like these were made by blowing balloons of glass. The balloon was spun round until it flattened out. (Look back to page 7 to give you an idea of how this was done.) The flat pieces of glass were then cut into the right shapes for windows. It was much harder to make big panes of glass.

▲ The lumps on these window panes are where the blowing tube was attached to the balloon of glass. You might see these windows in old houses.

Glass for lenses

Have you ever tried looking through glass that is curved? Try looking at some writing through a bottle or a jam jar. Move the bottle or jar up and down or from side to side. What happens to the letters?

Curved glass can make things look bigger, or smaller, or a different shape. Sometimes this can be very useful.

16

Magnifying lenses are made from curved glass. Feel one with your fingers. The glass bulges out in the middle. This kind of lens is called convex. It makes things look bigger.

Other lenses curve inwards. They are called concave lenses and they make things look smaller. Try looking through some different lenses. How thick are they? Which way do they curve? What can you see through them?

17

Have you ever been to the optician to have your eyes tested?

If he thinks you need glasses, the optician might give you a special pair of frames to try on. He has a box of different lenses and he can put the lenses into the frames to find out which ones help you to see better.

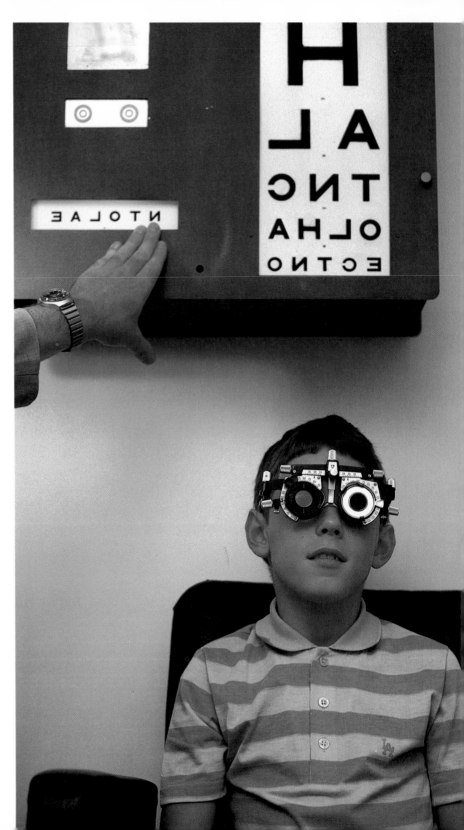

Each pair of glasses is specially made for the person who is going to wear them. The lenses have to be exactly the right thickness and curve in the right way. That's why you should never wear another person's glasses.

There are lenses inside cameras and binoculars, too. Can you think of any other things which have lenses inside them? Try to think of times when we need to make things look bigger or smaller.

Colored glass

This stained glass window is made from lots of different pieces of colored glass. It is especially beautiful when sunlight shines through it.

If you want to see how it works, try this.

You will need

A flashlight

A piece of white paper

Some different colored glass bottles

How to do it

Find a place where there isn't too much sunlight. Ask an adult to help you put the bottles in a row. Shine the flashlight through the first bottle. Hold the paper on the other side of the bottle so that the light goes on to it. What color is the light on the paper? Now try this with the other bottles.

See if you can visit a church or mosque that has a stained glass window. What color is the light that comes through the window?

Glass can be made in all sorts of different colors. Sometimes the color is mixed in when the glass is hot, so the glass is colored all the way through. Sometimes colors are painted on top of the glass. Have another look at the colored glass in your collection. Does the color go all the way through or is it painted on the glass?

You could try painting your own design on the windows of your classroom. Use water-based paint so that the design can be washed off.

21

Patterned glass

Glass comes in different patterns as well as different colors. See how many kinds of patterned glass you can find around your home or school.

Some patterns are cut into the glass ▶ to make it sparkle.

◀ Some patterns are scratched on to the glass.

Some patterns are ▶ stamped into the glass while it is hot.
Can you see that this is one small pattern, printed over and over again? It's called a repeated pattern. Try designing your own repeated pattern.

Toughened glass

If we treat glass carefully, we can usually make sure that it doesn't break. But sometimes glass needs to be made stronger so that it can be used for special jobs.

Car windows are made of a special kind of glass that doesn't break into sharp splinters.

Specially toughened glass is also used for large buildings like this one.

Ordinary glass would break if it was put into a hot oven. Some dishes are made of a different kind of glass that won't break if it gets very hot or cold.

Another kind of glass is used to store strong chemicals that might eat into ordinary glass and make holes in it.

Street lamps are made out of this kind of glass, too.

Can you think of any other things that are made out of toughened glass?

23

Glass and plastic

Lots of things that used to be made from glass are now made from plastic. Which do you think is better? Plastic doesn't break easily, but it can't be recycled as easily as glass. Try making a list of all the good things about plastic and all the good things about glass. How many objects can you find that are made out of plastic *and* out of glass?

Glass can be made into many beautiful things — even furniture — so it will probably be used for a long time to come.

More things to do

1. Different types of glass are made to do different jobs. Here are the five main types. Can you think of some different objects that could be made from each type of glass?
Soda-lime-silica glass is made from ingredients that are cheap and easy to find. The glass can be made in very large quantities and is easily melted and shaped. It is fairly tough, but won't stand up to extreme temperatures or hard knocks.
Brosilicate glass is made to withstand extreme temperatures.
Lead crystal glass sparkles very brightly and is easy to cut and engrave.
Optical glass is very pure and can be made into exact shapes and thicknesses.
Neutral glass is a mixture of soda-lime-silica glass and brosilicate glass. It is not eaten away by strong chemicals.

2. See if you can find a recycling center near your home. Why do you think it is divided into sections? Try to find out where the bottles are collected and where they go to.

3. Try making a glass musical instrument. Fill several bottles and drinking glasses with water and then *lightly* tap them with a pencil. What happens if you try different amounts of water in the same container?

4. Crystal Palace was a spectacular glass building, made for the Great Exhibition in London, England, 1851. It burned down in 1936. See if you can find a picture of it in your library and try to find out more about how it was built.

5. Try to work out how many square feet of glass have been used for the windows in your school.

6. Glass has been made and used for thousands of years. Find out if there is a museum near you where you can see glass objects that were made a long time ago.

7. Very thin strands of high-quality glass, called optical fibers, can be used to carry signals like telephone wires. See if you can find out more about how they are used.

Index